Motivational Strategies & Principles
to Keep your Light Shining

7-WEEK DEVOTIONAL

REV. MATTHEW SHANNON

Keep your Life LIT

Motivational Strategies &
Principles to Keep your Light Shining

7-Week Devotional

Rev. Matthew Shannon
Author

Ignite Your Core Publishing Company
Virginia Beach, VA
United States

Ignite Your Core Publishing

Copyright ©2020 Rev. Matthew Shannon
All rights reserved.

All rights reserved. This book is protected under the copyright laws of the United States of America. This book may not be copied or reprinted for commercial gain or profit. The use of short quotations, prayers, strategy questions and motivational thoughts may be copied for personal and small groups. For permissions for larger groups and other permissions, please email Ignite Your Core Publishing Company at: igniteyourcorepublishing@gmail.com

NRSV: "New Revised Standard Version Bible, © 1989, Division of Christian Education of the National Council of the Churches of Christ to the United States of America. Used by permission. All rights reserved.

MSG: Unless otherwise indicated, all Scripture quotations are taken from The Message, copyright © 1993, 2002, 2018 by Eugene H. Peterson. Used by permission of NavPress. All rights reserved. Represented by Tyndale House Publishers, a division of Tyndale House Ministries.

Printed in the United States of America.

ISBN: 978-1-7335736-0-3

Table of Contents

Week One - The Bushel Basket
Page 9

Week Two - Discard the Bushel Basket
Page 17

Week Three - Silence is not always Golden
Page 25

Week Four - Are you Afraid of your Own Light?
Page 33

Week Five - Living a LIT Life
Page 41

Week Six - Principles to Keep your Light Shining
Page 51

Week Seven - Keep your Life LIT
Page 65

Bonus: Week Eight - Your Response
Page 73

This devotional is dedicated to the people whose lives will be changed after applying the strategic principles within this book to their life.

Introduction to Keep your Life LIT

"It is you who light my lamp; the Lord, my God, lights up my darkness." – Psalm 18:28 (NRSV)

Are you afraid to be in the dark? People who don't like the dark have a source of light, either a lamp, a flashlight, or a candle. Some people have dimmer switches to control the brightness of the light. However, you don't want to dim the light that God has placed inside of you. Fear, stress, hate, procrastination and the enemy want to control the brightness of your light. You can't allow this to happen. **You have to keep your life LIT!**

"Lit" used to mean getting drunk a century ago. Now, "lit" means to be excellent or exciting. In this devotional, "lit" means light, excellent, and exciting. Over the next seven weeks, you will learn how to identify your spiritual bushel baskets, how to discard and remove them, how to live a lit life and how to keep your life lit. In each week, there are strategy questions, a prayer, and a motivational thought designed to help you to apply what you have learned to your life. It's possible that you could read the book in thirty minutes, but that won't benefit you. The best way to read this devotional is to read for the week, meditate, strategize, act and repeat until you are finished. Track the changes that God makes in your life.

Keep your Life Lit!

Week One
The Bushel Basket

"No one after lighting a lamp puts it under the bushel basket..."
Matthew 5:15a

During late August, into September and October, apples are ripe for picking at the apple orchards. I remember visiting an apple orchard in Winchester, Virginia in September 2017. One of the items that I received to pick my apples was a bushel basket. I filled the bushel basket with green apples, red apples, sweet apples, small and large apples. The bushel basket achieved its purpose. It had carried all of my apples until I reached the checkout line. At the checkout line, I exchanged my bushel basket for a plastic bag. I left the apple orchard with an exciting experience, but with disappointment that I couldn't keep my bushel basket. I had to leave it at the apple orchard.

In the gospel of St. Matthew, chapter 5, Jesus is preaching to his disciples on a mountain. This chapter is known as the Sermon on the Mount. One of the illustrations Jesus uses is the idea that no one after lighting a lamp puts it under the bushel basket. The purpose of the bushel basket in this sense is to cover the light of the lamp. Jesus states that no one does this! In a spiritual sense, why do you place a bushel basket over your own light?

The spiritual bushel basket is anything or anyone that prevents your light from shining. Do you have any bushel baskets in your life? Some spiritual bushel baskets are fear, doubt, hate, procrastination, self-pity, jealousy, greed, lust, self-limitations, anxiety, and stress. Spiritual bushel baskets cover the light that God has placed inside of you. Bushel baskets are cover ups! Sometimes, cover ups are easy to get comfortable with.

Fear is a cover up for courage, doubt is a cover up for faith, and hate is a cover up for love. Here is a closer look at how procrastination, self-pity, and jealousy are cover ups.

It's easy to procrastinate. However, if you procrastinate, you forfeit the "right now moment" for the uncertainty of tomorrow. This will inevitably delay your light from shining. Someone might need to see your light shine, but you are preventing it from happening. You are possibly waiting for a moment that will never arrive. Write the book, start the nonprofit organization, go to school, take steps to get out of debt, make a difference in someone's life, Tomorrow is not promised!

Another example of someone placing a bushel basket over their light was Naomi in the first chapter of Ruth. Naomi lost her husband and her two sons. All she had left in her family was her two daughters-in-law Ruth and Orpah. Naomi started to push away her daughters-in-law. She told them to go back home and to let her be. Naomi suffered from self-pity. Naomi was a great person, but she allowed death and grief to send her into self-pity. The bushel basket of self-pity covered Naomi's light temporarily. God sent Ruth into Naomi's life to walk the journey with her. Ruth told her, *"Do not press me to leave you or to turn back from following you! Where you go, I will go; where you lodge, I will lodge; your people shall be my people, and your God my God. Where you die, I will die—there will I be buried. May the Lord do this and so to me and more as well, if even death parts me from you!"* Naomi had nothing else to say to her. Naomi realized she couldn't push Ruth away. Naomi had to let her light shine for Ruth.

Jealousy is a bushel basket over what God has in store for you. When you are jealous of someone's possessions or their relationships, you are denying yourself of what God has blessed you with. In Genesis 37, Joseph told his brothers his dreams that one day, he would rule over them. Joseph's brothers envied him, so they put him in a pit. They placed Joseph in a pit hoping that his dream would never be fulfilled. Joseph's brothers' jealousy prevented them from seeing their light. Instead, they wanted to stop Joseph's light from shining. Watch out for people who are jealous of your dreams, your gifts, and your relationships. They will attempt to cover up your light because they are looking for the light within their own inner being.

Greed is a cover up for cheerful giving. Lust is a cover up for a real loving relationship. Self-limitation is a cover up for doing the impossible. Anxiety and stress are cover ups for trusting in God. Proverbs 3:5-6 declares, Trust in the Lord with all thine heart, lean not unto thine own understanding. In all thy ways acknowledge him and he shall direct thy paths.

The enemy desires you to have these bushel baskets over your light. As long as your light doesn't shine, the devil wins. As long as your light is hidden, the enemy is comfortable because it is dark. The enemy enjoys watching you not living in your God-given potential. It's time for you to release the bushel baskets, the cover ups over your light! Your life deserves to be lit!

Strategy Questions:

Which bushel baskets have you placed over your light?

_____

_____

_____

_____

Jesus told his disciples that they were the light of the world. If you are the light in the world, why have you placed a bushel basket over your light?

_____

_____

_____

_____

Prayer

God, help me to identify the bushel baskets that are over my light. No one lights a lamp and puts a bushel basket over it. In Jesus name, I pray. Amen.

Week One Motivational Thought

Spiritual Bushel Baskets are cover-ups for your God-given destiny.

Week Two
Discard the Bushel Basket

"Lay aside every weight and the sin that clings so closely…"

Hebrews 12:1 (NRSV)

Every day in the United States, people throw out tons of food, plastic water bottles, and other items of waste. Some things that people throw away sit in the landfill for years trying to decompose. Conversely, there are some people that don't like to throw anything away. I saw the inside of someone's house once and it looked like they didn't throw anything away. I could hardly walk or sit down. I wondered to myself, how could a person live like this?

In the previous chapter, you learned about the spiritual bushel basket. In order to live a life that is lit, you have to discard the bushel baskets in your life. You won't have a lit life keeping around fear, doubt, hate, procrastination, self-pity, greed, jealously, lust, anxiety and stress. The writer of Hebrews 12:1, instructs believers to lay aside every weight, the sin that is so close to the believer. What sins are close to you? What sins do you need to discard?

Once you identify your personal spiritual bushel baskets, then you have to take the steps to lay them aside and throw them away. There are three strategies that will help you to throw away these baskets. They are to: love yourself, self-discipline, and being courageous.

Before you can love others, you have to love yourself first. The second greatest commandment that Jesus told his disciples was to love your neighbors as you love yourself. What does loving yourself require? Loving you is putting your well-being near the front. Loving you requires that you take care of your inner being. It's easy to care for others, while neglecting you. I have seen caregivers spend their time looking out for the people they care for, while putting themselves on the backburner. They will feed the hungry, clothe the naked, and give water to those who are thirsty. Meanwhile, they themselves are hungry, not clothed, and are thirsty. I have seen countless times where the caregiver dies first and their patient lives on. Why does this happen? In order to help someone else, we have to help ourselves first. We are blessed to be a blessing. How can you be a blessing if you have not been blessed? How can you expend energy if you are lacking energy? The key to being lit is loving you. How do you do that? Loving you requires that you speak positive things to yourself, that you give yourself permission to dream and bring into reality your dream, that you spend time taking an inventory of your spirit, and that you release the pressure from being perfect. It is very important to take care and love your light. God made your light! Love it, don't' compare your light with others! Your light might be in education, while another light maybe in sports, but each light serves a higher purpose in God's Kingdom. Learn how to love your light!

One of the characteristics described as one of the fruit of the spirit is self-control or self-discipline. Self-discipline is the ability to control your decisions, actions and response to the environment around you. Self-discipline is the innate ability to control your emotion, overcome any weaknesses and to resist the urge to make bad choices. Having self-discipline will help you to discard your spiritual bushel baskets. The baskets over your light are your weaknesses and it can cause you to make bad choices or respond to a situation that is not your best. If you use self-discipline you can disarm your baskets over your light. If you are in a worrisome situation, you don't have to respond in doubt. You can choose to respond with faith and have trust in God. If you find yourself suffering with lack, you don't have to respond with self-pity. You can choose to trust in God's Word, that God will supply all of your needs according to God's riches in glory. You can look for God's opportunities for provision. Be proactive in discovering God's providing power in your life.

The third characteristic that you need to discard the baskets in the way of your light is courage. Being strong and courageous is an instruction that God gave to Moses successor, Joshua. God told Joshua to be strong and courageous three times.

Joshua 1: 6,7, 9 says, "Be strong and courageous; for you shall put this people in possession of the land that I swore to their ancestors to give them. Only be strong and very courageous, being careful to act in accordance with all the law that my servant Moses commanded you; do not turn from it to the right hand or to the left, so that you may be successful wherever you go. I hereby command you: Be strong and courageous; do not be frightened or dismayed, for the Lord your God is with you wherever you go." (NRSV)

God knew that Joshua and the Israelites would face some fierce opponents in battle and would have to face their inner doubts and fears at the same time. They no longer had the comfort of Moses' staff to declare them victory. The Israelites had to rely on themselves and God's power. God's power in Joshua's life would only be activated if he was strong and courageous. In addition, Joshua had to be obedient to the commands of the Lord. Joshua did not allow his fear to stop him from defeating his opponents. This is what you must do.

You don't have to fear. Psalms 27:1 says, The Lord is my light and my salvation, whom shall I fear? (NRSV) When you are in a scary situation, you don't have to respond in fear. You can choose to respond with an attitude of bravery and courage. God's light is on your side as long as you have faith and trust in God. Be brave, be strong, and be courageous and you will watch yourself discarding the spiritual bushel baskets over your light!

Strategy Questions:

Which strategy do you have the most difficulty with? How will you improve on loving you, having self-discipline, or being courageous?

_____

_____

_____

What steps will you take to discard the spiritual bushel baskets over your light?

_____

_____

_____

Prayer

God, I am going to be proactive in recognizing and discarding the bushel baskets that are over my light. Assist me as I develop steps to discard them. In Jesus name, I pray. AMEN.

Week Two Motivational Thought

I will love me, watch how I respond to my environment and be courageous.

Week Three
Silence is not always Golden

"Our lives begin to end the day we become silent about things that matter."
The Rev. Dr. Martin L. King, Jr.

There is a saying that goes, silence is golden. However, this isn't always the case. As I was growing up, people often told me that I was quiet, shy, and non-talkative. One person even wondered if I was paying attention because I didn't talk much. I would always respond to these comments by saying, if you talk to me, I'll talk to you. Additionally, I would say if I'm not talking, I'm either listening or observing. However, over the years, I have learned that something's I can't be silent about. When it comes to God, you can't be silent. When it comes to the mistreatment of God's people, you can't be silent. Now, there are some battles, I learned to let the

Lord fight, while other battles I decide to say something. I too often see when a crime is committed, no one will say if they saw anything or not. Sometimes, people are scared to speak up for fear of retaliation. Fear is one of the main reasons people choose to stay silent and not speak up. Silence is not always golden.

When King Nebuchadnezzar threatened the three Hebrew boys to worship his statue or else he would throw them thrown into a fiery furnace, they didn't remain silent. The three Hebrew boys spoke up to King Nebuchadnezzar, because serving and worshipping their God mattered to them. If the three Hebrew boys would have stayed silent, they would have abandoned the God they trusted. So, the choice is yours. It is your decision to speak up to the things that matter to you. Only you know what truly matters to you. Some people may not be offended at the same things you are. You can not depend on others to speak up for you! You have to speak for yourself!

So, the real question to you is: will you continue to be silent about the things that matter to you? We have seen in the last few years' different protests to different things. Some groups protest racism, police brutality(#BlackLivesMatter), sexual assault (#MeToo movement), women's rights, LGBTQ rights, equal pay or an increase in their pay on their jobs, gun rights or gun laws (#MarchforOurLives). The people in these groups have decided to make their voices heard. They have chosen to speak up for the causes that are important to them. Will you choose to speak up to the injustices that you believe are important and that matter? Whatever you do, you can't be silent about things that matter.

Your life's purpose is dependent on what you will speak to. One day, Jesus saw a woman that was about to be stoned to death because she was accused of committing adultery. Jesus stepped beside the woman and told the people that were going to stone her, "You that are without sin cast the first stone." The people could not stone her. Jesus saved the woman's life and told her to sin no more. The point is, Jesus used his voice. This woman mattered to Jesus. Jesus could have easily passed by. Jesus is a person of love and compassion. This is why he had to speak up. Jesus could not remain silent because his purpose depended on it. Jesus came to give life more abundantly. Jesus came to forgive the world of its sins. His purpose demanded him to speak up.

Silence is not always golden. God is waiting on you to speak up for the brokenhearted, for the oppressed, for the poor, for the marginalized. God is waiting for you to decide what matters to you. There is a saying, "If you don't stand for anything, you will fall for everything." So, investigate your mind, your heart, and your soul for what matters to you. It is in this, that you will discover the true light that God has placed inside of you. There are seasons when you need to be silent, but there are also seasons when you have to speak up. Your light depends on you to speak up! If you speak up, God will back you up! God is able to protect you. Remember, you are strong and courageous. God is with you! Be bold and speak up! Silence is not always golden.

Strategy Questions:

List the causes that matter to you. How often do you speak up for these matters?

_____

_____

_____

_____

What stops you from speaking up?

_____

_____

_____

_____

Prayer

God, remove the hindrances that keep me silent about things that matter. My voice is important to someone. My voice can liberate someone, heal someone, teach someone, and my voice can lead a person to salvation. Help me to speak to things that matter. In Jesus name, I pray. AMEN.

Week Three Motivational Thought

Speak up against the injustices of this world!

Week Four
Are you Afraid of your Own Light?

"Our deepest fear is not that we are inadequate. Our deepest fear is that we are powerful beyond measure. It is our light, not our darkness, that most frightens us.
We ask ourselves, Who am I to be brilliant, gorgeous, talented, fabulous?
Actually, who are you not to be? You are a child of God.
Your playing small, does not serve the world. There's nothing enlightened about shrinking. So that other people won't feel insecure around you. We are all meant to shine, as children do. We were born to make manifest. The glory of God that is within us. It's not just in some of us; it's in everyone. And as we let our own light shine, we unconsciously give other people permission to do the same. As we're liberated from our own fear, our presence automatically liberates others."

Our Greatest Fear- Marianne Williamson

When I was 17 or 18, I remember driving my mother's Toyota Camry one afternoon. The sun was shining. My mother and my older sister were in the car. There was an older gentleman (maybe he was in his late 70's or 80's) driving a car in front of us. Our car has automatic running lights that stay on all the time. We can't turn them off. So, this gentleman driving in front of us slows down and gets in the left lane. We were driving right beside him. He rolls down his passenger window and boldly states, "Your lights are blinding me! Turn them off. Your lights are blinding me." After he said this, I thought to myself, how could my running lights blind you? There is no way that I can turn them down to ease your eyes. I have to leave them on, I have no option to cut my lights off.

Lights can blind us, scare us, and eradicate darkness from our lives. It's easy to be in awe or scared of someone else's light. Too often though, we are afraid of our own light. As Marianne Williamson stated, our deepest fear is that we are powerful beyond measure…It is our light, not our darkness, that most frightens us.

So, are you afraid of your own light? Are you afraid of the difference your light will make in the world? Your light is powerful, it is bright. Your light is supposed to shine in darkness. Your light is supposed to shine during the day. You don't have to be scared of the great power that is within you. Some people don't launch their careers because they are scared of the success that might happen. Some people don't write the book, record the podcast, or start the business, because they are afraid that it will make a difference and that it will grow way beyond them. This vulnerability of shining our light so others might see, is so frightening! You might think: Is my light good enough? Is my light worth sharing? What if people reject my light? These thoughts are completely normal. Just because you have these thoughts, don't let it stop you. Proverbs 16:3-4a says, "Commit your work to the Lord, and your plans will be established. The Lord has made everything for its purpose." (NRSV) See, God created your light. It shines with others, but your light serves a unique purpose. No one else has a light exactly like yours. When you don't share yours because of fear, it strips the world an opportunity to see in the midst of darkness. "One of you puts to flight a thousand, since it is the Lord your God who fights for you." - Joshua 23:10 (NRSV)

There is no need to fear your light because God is right there with you. God's Word is a light unto your path. God will never leave you or forsake you. If you let God guide your light, you don't' have to fear your own light.

When you share your light, people will see that it's okay to share theirs, too. Do you remember the #MeToo movement? What made this powerful was that one person told their story and it empowered others to share their story. Well, that's how powerful your light is. Don't let fear stop you from shining and sharing. The Creator made you good enough to shine. The Creator will guide you through your success. Someone is waiting for you to dance, waiting for you to write a song, waiting for you to accept your call to ministry, waiting for you to finish the book, record the podcast, start the business, start the non-profit, finish the degree, buy the home, or start the family. If you don't know who's waiting, its you! It's time to focus on what God has placed inside of you. Stop looking around and praying that someone else will do it for you. This is your moment. This is your day, your time to shine! Don't worry about letting your real light shine. You are going to have people that will try to smother your light, but don't focus on them. Strip fear and focus on God's light and your light, and your light will do the impossible!

Strategy Questions:

What is your greatest fear about sharing your own light?

_____

_____

_____

_____

What steps will you take to strip fear off of your light?

_____

_____

_____

_____

Prayer

To the Guiding Light of my Salvation, please assist me to strip fear away from my light. God, you created my unique light for a purpose. Shine bright on the path that I must follow. God, my light is good enough to share. It is powerful beyond measure, don't let me shrink or dim my light, so that I can please other's insecurities and judgements. In Your Son's Liberating Name, Jesus, I pray. AMEN.

Week Four Motivational Thought

Strip the fear off your powerful light and let it shine!

Week Five
Living a LIT Life

"For you were once in darkness, but now in the Lord you are light. Live as children of light---for the fruit of the light is found in all that is good and right and true."

Ephesians 5:8-9 (NRSV)

After identifying and discarding the spiritual bushel baskets over your light, it's time to start living a lit life. How do you this and what does this process look like? Well, first, you have to remove the temptation to pick up the bushel basket again. You don't ever want to dim your light again. So, you have to release the spiritual bushel basket with CARE. CARE is Counsel, Action, Refresh, & Exceed expectations.

It's time to release fear, stress, doubt, lack of acceptance with CARE. It's time to release the people, the places, and things that stop you from living a lit life with CARE.

CARE begins with Counsel. It's important that you seek wise counsel in removing the dimmer of your spiritual light. The prophet Isaiah calls Jesus, the Wonderful Counselor. Counselor is "yaats" in the Hebrew root form and "yowes" in the Hebrew original form. It means to seek advice, to seek counsel. King David listened to the counsel of his friend Nathan. In the aftermath of the murder of Uriah, the pregnancy of Bathsheba, and the adulterous act of David; Nathan had to counsel David on his misdoings. Nathan convinced David to become clean of his guilt. The acts that David did had the potential to diminish his light, but because David listened to wise counsel, these events didn't stand a chance. Seeking counsel doesn't mean you are crazy, it just means you need another set of unbiased eyes and ears. Counselors can see things you can't. There are all kinds of counselors: mental health, sexual, substance abuse, family and marriage, career guidance, and rehabilitation. Whatever is stopping your light, please seek counsel to remove it. The hymn writer, Doris Akers, wrote these words, "Lead me, guide me along the way; For if you lead me, I cannot stray; Lord, let me walk each day with Thee. Lead me, O Lord, lead me." Without the Wonderful Counselor, you are lost, without his guidance, you are misdirected. Seek Wise Counsel!

The A in CARE is for Action. James 2:17 says, "So faith by itself, if it has no works, is dead." When releasing your spiritual bushel basket, action is required. You have to do something. It simply won't go away. You have to put in some work to get it removed. As noted in Week 2, you can simply discard the bushel basket over your light. How will you do it? The wise counsel told you what to do, will you do it? If your addiction is keeping you from you shining your light, how will you stop your addiction? With God, It's possible! For example, if you are addicted to social media and it is stopping you from who God called you to be, it's time to act. Maybe you develop an action plan, and start with deactivating one social media account for one day, then work up to a week. While you aren't on social media, you can focus on shining your light—writing the song, being in community (real people), or volunteering for a nonprofit---This is action! Remember, one small act can lead to bigger acts. Don't despise small steps. They are critical to your journey. Act and remove the spiritual bushel basket.

The R in CARE is for Refresh. Refresh means to give new strength or energy to; to reinvigorate. Things and people that dim your light don't need your energy or strength anymore. It's time to hit refresh on your life and light. Refresh your body, your mind, and your soul. When you refresh, people will look at you differently. You will see situations differently. Ephesians 5:8, is important right here. For you were once in darkness, but now in the Lord you are light. When you start living a lit life after being in the dark for so long, you will feel refreshed, reinvigorated. Maybe you were living a lit life, but stopped because of burnout, depression, loneliness, or stress. Take this opportunity now, let Christ light your light again. Jesus spoke, "Come to me, all that are weary and are carrying heavy burdens, and I will give you rest."- Matthew 11:28 (NRSV) Being rested and refreshed is critical to sharing your light to the world. I'm going to be real right here, sometimes I don't feel like fulfilling my calling because I'm tired. It's in these moments, I pause and allow God to refresh me. God's presence will refresh you. I know that fatigue and weariness can be a spiritual bushel basket. Sometimes, we think that pastors, singers, celebrities, entertainers, parents, teachers, doctors, and more have an endless supply of energy. That's not the case. Weariness will dim your light if you allow it. Don't allow it! Rest, so God can refresh you. That's the purpose of sleep…sleep allows God the opportunity to refresh your body, your mind, your light, your soul for a brand new day.

Once you're refreshed, you are ready for E. The E in CARE is for Exceeding expectations. When you were living with a dimmed to non-existent light, no one expected anything from you. You didn't expect anything from you. Now, that you are living a lit life, it's time to exceed your own expectations. How is this possible? When you are living a lit life with Jesus, your light becomes even brighter. Ephesians 3:20 states, "Now to him who by the power at work within us is able to accomplish abundantly far more than all we can ask or imagine." (NRSV) Did you hear that? Did you read that? Now to him who by the power at work within us…when we live a lit life with Jesus, Jesus will be able to accomplish far more than we can ask or imagine. So, you can exceed expectations. Let God in while you are creating, volunteering, and assisting and your light will travel farther than your vision board and definitely farther than what you can do on your own. Exceed your expectations!

It's time to live a lit life. No more hiding, we have released those spiritual bushel baskets with CARE. Living a lit life is the best thing you can do. What does living a lit life look like? Well, it's letting your light shine consistently. It's following this command: So let us not grow weary in doing what is right, for we will reap at harvest time, if we do not give up. – Galatians 6:9 (NRSV) Live a LIT life!

Strategy Questions:

Identify the spiritual bushel baskets that you need counsel and an action plan to remove. Create a counseling and action plan.

How often do you allow God to refresh you? Create a plan to let God refresh you even more.

What are your expectations for your lit life?

Prayer

Dear God, it's time for me to take the next step and live a lit life. Help me to release my spiritual bushel baskets with CARE. Place wise counselors in my life. I realize action is necessary to walk in your light. Refresh me, when weariness and tiredness come to dim my light. With you, I can exceed my expectations. I want to live a LIT life, in Jesus name, I pray. AMEN.

Week Five Motivational Thought

Live a lit life with God as your guide and your light will impact more than you can plan, think, or imagine.

Week Six
Principles to Keep your Light Shining

"The fruit of the Spirit is love, joy, peace, patience, kindness, generosity, faithfulness, gentleness, and self-control."

Galatians 5:22-23 (NRSV)

The enemy will tempt you to go back and live a dim life, but these are the principles that will help you to keep your light shining. The following principles aren't listed in any particular order. It's not like a college class, where you might need a prerequisite.

Principle #1- Service

The greatest among you will be your servant. – Matthew 23:11 (NRSV) Dr. Martin Luther King, Jr. stated, "Everyone can be great…because anybody can serve." Service is an important principle that will keep your light shining. Service doesn't have to cost you money. It can be as simple as volunteering at a homeless shelter or a clothes closet. It could be creating blessing bags to give to the less fortunate. It could be teaching a computer/technology class to a group of senior citizens or those unfamiliar with technology. You could share a smile to someone who is dealing with tough circumstances. You could cook a meal for someone who is paying an expensive student loan. There are many more ways that you can serve. Service requires that you are thinking about others before yourself. When you serve, your light will keep shining and you will be great.

Principle #2- Compassion

As God's chosen ones, holy and beloved, clothe yourselves with compassion...- Colossians 3:12 (NRSV)

Compassion is the concern for the sufferings or misfortunes of others. You can find multiple times within the gospels, Christ shined his light with compassion. One instance of this happens in Matthew 15:32. Jesus called his disciples to him and said, "I have compassion for the crowd, because they have been with me now for three days and have nothing to eat; and I do not want to send them away hungry, for they might faint on the way." (NRSV) Jesus had compassion for the hungry. He wanted to make sure they were fed, so they could stay healthy. Have you been compassionate towards your neighbors? Sometimes, people make fun of people who are going through a hard time or they judge them. God wants us to have compassion just like the Good Samaritan. People (a priest and a Levite) that should have helped the hurting man, didn't. The one who should have passed by (Samaritan), stopped and gave relief to the hurting man. The

Good Samaritan let his light shine. Having compassion for others will keep your light shining.

Principle #3- Patience

If we hope for what we do not see, we wait for it with patience. – Romans 8:25 (NRSV)

We live in a fast-paced world. It seems like everyone wants things in a hurry. If you're driving on a highway with a speed limit of 55-60mph, almost no one drives that. Some speed by doing 75 mph and higher. People are always looking for a quick meal. The millennial and Xer's generation have quick attention spans; they read the news in 140 characters or less. Quick is not always the best. The bible says, the race is not given to the swift, but the ones who can endure. Life is not a sprint; it is a journey. You have to have patience. Patience is having the ability to accept delay or setbacks without getting angry or upset.

Good things come to those who have patience. When you obtain patience, you will release the necessity to rush things. You will begin to accept that God operates in God's time, not your own time. Rushing will cause accidents, but having patience will help you to avoid accidents and giving up prematurely. Developing patience in your life, will help you to become patient with others. You will receive the reward of seeing a person develop from an unbeliever to an authentic Christian. Wait on the Lord, and be of good courage! Patience will keep your light shining.

Principle #4- Having a Standard / Character

If you don't stand for something, you will fall for anything. Having a standard, character, or integrity will help keep your light shining. You can accomplish great things, but if your character is flawed, your actions will be in vain. The content of your character is crucial in maintaining your light. Maya Angelou once stated, "I've learned that people will forget what you said, people will forget what you did, but people will never forget how you made them feel." Treat your character with respect. "Character creates a foundation upon which the structure of your talent and your life can build. If there are cracks in that foundation, you cannot build much."- John Maxwell.[1] Having character and integrity opens doors for you and draws boundaries for you on what you will and will not do. A positive character will help you keep a good name. "A good name is to be chosen rather than great riches, and favor is better than silver or gold." – Proverbs 22:1 (NRSV) Keep character around and your light will continue to shine.

Principle #5- Persistence

There are blessings that come because you are persistent. There was a widow who was seeking justice from an unfair and uncompassionate judge. The widow went to see the judge every day with her request. Eventually, the judge got so bothered by the widow's presence constantly, he gave her justice against her opponent. The unfair judge said, "Though I have no fear of God and no respect for anyone, yet because this widow keeps bothering me, I will grant her justice, so that she may not wear me out by continually coming." – Luke 18:4-5 (NRSV) If persistence can cause a judge to change his attitude, what can persistence do in your life. If you keep praying, God will answer your prayer. In the same way, persistence will keep your light shining. Stay lit no matter the opponents or obstacles that come to turn off your light. Your light shines with persistence.

Principle #6- Kindness

"I led them with cords of human kindness, with bands of love. I was to them like those who lift infants to their cheeks. I bent down to them and fed them." Hosea 11:4 (NRSV)

When you think of someone who is kind, what do they do? Some people express kindness by sharing a hug, sending a card, paying for a meal, offering a word of encouragement, or expressing empathy in times of loss and pain. Kindness is a positive trait to have. You will attract more people in your life when you are kind. When someone is kind to you, you feel good. You remember their act of kindness. Be kind towards your enemies. I remember this slogan: Kill them with kindness. When you are kind to someone, you allow your light to shine. The world needs more kindness. With the constant social media bullying, the world needs more people to be kind. Kindness will keep your light shining.

Principle #7- Faith

"If you have faith the size of a mustard seed, you will say to this mountain, 'Move from here to there,' and it will move; and nothing will be impossible for you." Matthew 17:20 (NRSV)

The principle of faith is vital for you, if you want your light to shine. On more than multiple occasions, people in the gospels were healed because of their faith. Demons were cast out because of faith. There is a whole list of heroes and sheroes in Hebrews 11 who used faith…Noah, Abel, Enoch, Abraham, Isaac, Jacob, Rahab, and more. Faith was used to conquer kingdoms, administer justice, obtain promises, shut the mouths of lions, won strength out of weakness, and put foreign armies to flight. You will go nowhere without faith. Faith is believing the unseen. With faith, you can turn impossible to possible. With faith, you can pay off your student loan debt. With faith in God, you can turn a cancer diagnosis into a complete restoration of your body. Faith can take you places. Faith sees the door and walks through it. You don't need much of it either. You only need to believe a little bit and you can move mountains. Faith will keep your light shining, if you believe it will. Declare right now, my light will keep shining!

Principle #8- Hope

My hope is built on nothing less than Jesus blood and righteousness, I dare not trust the sweetest frame, but wholly lean on Jesus name. On Christ the solid rock, I stand, all other ground is sinking sand.[2] These are the lyrics to one of my favorite hymns. When trials and tribulations arrive on your doorstep, you need hope to overcome them. If you lose this principle of hope, you have nearly lost everything. Don't fear if you become hopeless. God gives hope to the hopeless. Hope is a feeling of expectation and desire for something to happen. When you place your hope in God, you expect God will do something in your life. God gives us a hope for the future. Hope will keep your light shining because sometimes there will be some days and nights, that is all you will have is hope. Hope says there is a chance. Hope says it's not over! Hope says I think I can. When you are going through tough times, hold on to your hope in Jesus. He will pull you through.

Principle #9- Love

Faith, hope, and love, but the greatest of these is love.[3] You can have all the previous eight principles, but if you do not have love, you gain nothing. Your light won't shine. So, if there is a prerequisite, it would be the principle of love. Love is the root of all the other principles. God is love. In Paul's love chapter, 1st Corinthians 13, it says that love is patient and kind. Love does not envy, boast, or keep a record of wrongs. Love bears all things, hopes all things. There is no end to love. It was love that God had for you to send his only begotten Son, so that you might believe and have eternal life. It was love that kept Jesus on the cross to pay the ultimate price for your sin. Love is powerful. The type of love that will keep your light shining is Agape love. This type of love is unconditional. It doesn't depend on conditions or circumstances. This is the love that God calls you to show. This is the love that Jesus refers to when he says, "Love your enemies." Agape love suffers inconvenience and discomfort for the benefit of another without expecting anything in return.[4] Love is not an easy task, but it is essential for your light to keep shining.

Strategy Questions:

Which of these principles mentioned do you need to work on and improve?

Are there any additional principles that will help keep your light shining?

Prayer

Thank you God for revealing to me the principles that will help keep my light shining. I understand that the root of these principles is love. If I don't have love, I gain nothing. If I hate my brother or sister, I am still in darkness. God, help me to discover the agape love within my heart, so that I can share it with others. In Jesus name, I pray. AMEN.

Week Six Motivational Thought

Keep your light shining with service, compassion, patience, character, persistence, kindness, faith, hope, and most importantly love.

Week Seven
Keep your Life LIT

"Darkness cannot drive out darkness, only light can do that." – Martin L. King, Jr.

So, far you have learned how to discard your spiritual bushel baskets, how to speak up for the voiceless, and the principles that will help you keep your light shining. Now, you will discover why it is important to keep your life lit. You will learn about people in the bible that kept their life lit.

John 3:19-21 (NRSV) says, "And this is the judgment, that the light has come into the world, and people loved darkness rather than light because their deeds were evil. For all who do evil hate the light and do not come to the light, so that their deeds may not be exposed. But those who do what is true come to the light, so that it may be clearly seen that their deeds have been done in God."

The purpose of keeping your life lit is this: Consistently doing great and positive deeds that will expose the truth, drive away darkness, and glorifying your God in heaven. When you keep your life lit, the world will see your light. The Message Bible says it this way, "Now that I've put you on the hilltop, on a light stand-shine... By opening up to others, you'll prompt people to open up with God, this generous Father in heaven." Matthew 5:14-16 (The Message)

Keeping your life lit will consistently inspire others to get their lives lit. One great deed that is available to all, is saying yes to salvation. When you are saved, you inspire others to be saved. Likewise, when you finish the book, your book will inspire others to great and awesome deeds. Your life lit will help other lives to be lit.

Some examples of lives that were lit in the Bible are: the three Hebrew boys, Rahab, David, Peter, Paul, and Jesus. The three Hebrew boys stood up to King Nebuchadnezzar. They defiantly told the King that they would not serve or worship any idol god. King Nebuchadnezzar put them into a fiery furnace, the Hebrew boys did not die, but were saved by an unknown fourth man. God had come through to save the Hebrew boys. Their lit life saved not only themselves but King Nebuchadnezzar, too. "Therefore, I (King Nebuchadnezzar) make a decree: Any people, nation, or language that utters blasphemy against the God of Shadrach, Meshach, and Abednego shall be torn limb from limb, and their houses laid in ruins; for there is no other god who is able to deliver in this way." Daniel 3:29 (NRSV). Likewise, Rahab lived a lit life too. Rahab hid Joshua's spies in her house away from the king of Jericho. This great deed led to this: "The men said to her, 'Our life for yours! If you do not tell this business of ours, then we will deal kindly and faithfully with you when the Lord gives us land." Joshua

2:14 (NRSV) Rahab's lit life lead the spies to be kind to her as well. David's life was lit despite his negative actions (murder, lying, and adultery). David laid the foundation for the temple to be built. David gathered the materials needed and found a location. This deed helped his son, Solomon build the temple for God. By the way, Solomon's mother was Bathsheba. It's interesting how God turned that around. Peter's life was lit. Peter, most known for denying Jesus three times, did a great deed after the Holy Spirit descended upon the disciples in Acts. Peter shared the first gospel message and extended the first invitation to Christ. The early church was formed. Over 3,000 people were saved that day. People were added to the number daily. Peter's lit life prompted people to begin their journey with Christ. Over 2,000 years later, we still worship in church! Another biblical witness to live a lit life was Paul, formerly known as Saul. Paul's great deed came through his writing. He wrote letters to the churches of Rome, Corinth, Ephesus, Thessalonica, Galatia, Philippi, and Colossae. Paul mentored and wrote letters to Timothy, Titus, and his friend Philemon. Through Paul's writings, people understand and can learn more about the Christian faith. Paul's lit life has led many to come to Christ. This last biblical witness of living a lit life is Jesus. Jesus did so many great deeds, there are too many to include in this book. One great deed that he did was to endure the cross of Calvary and die for our sins. Jesus submitted under the power of death for three days until God's spirit raised him from the dead. Through this great deed, Jesus has saved many lives. Jesus can become the center of your joy. Jesus is the reason why your life can be lit in the first place. Jesus' lit life brought glory to God, exposed the truth to the Pharisees and Sadducees, and drove away darkness (the devil). This is what you are now challenged to do with the light that is within you. Live a lit life. Most importantly, keep your life lit!

Strategy Questions:

Who do you know that lives a lit life? Are there any additional biblical witnesses?

_____

_____

_____

_____

How will you keep your life lit?

_____

_____

_____

_____

Prayer

God, keep my life lit so that I can be an inspiration for others. Protect my light, so that my light can drive out darkness and reveal the truth. Lead me to one good deed every day. In Jesus name I pray. AMEN.

Week Seven Motivational Thought

I'm keeping a LIT life to make a difference and bring glory to God.

Bonus Week Eight
Your Response

This is the message we have heard from him and proclaim to you, that God is light and in him there is no darkness at all. If we say that we have fellowship with him while we are walking in darkness, we lie and do not do what is true; but if we walk in the light as he himself is in the light, we have fellowship with one another, and the blood of Jesus his Son cleanses us from all sin.

1st John 1:5-7 (NRSV)

This week is just for you. There is nothing else to study. This is week is for you to apply what you have learned. It is for you to formulate and create a plan that will keep your life lit.

There is only one strategy question: What good works will you do to keep your life lit?

List your good works here and list how often you plan to do them. Explain how these good works will drive out darkness, expose truth, or prompt others to come to the light.

Prayer

Thank you, God for helping me to learn how to keep my life lit. Assist me in fulfilling this plan. In Jesus name, I pray. AMEN.

Week Eight Motivational Thought

This little light of mine, I'm gonna let it shine. Everywhere I go, I'm gonna let it shine. Jesus gave it to me, I'm gonna let it shine.

*Keep your Life Lit! *

References

1 Company, The John Maxwell (2013, March 11) John Maxwell. *Going Beyond Talent: Four Cores of Character.* Retrieved from https://www.johnmaxwell.com/blog/going-beyond-talent-four-cores-of-character/

2 Mote, Edward. (1834) My Hope is Built on Nothing Less.

3. Based on 1st Corinthians 13:13 (NRSV)

4 Truth, Compelling (2019, December 15) *What is the meaning of agape love?* Retrieved from https://www.compellingtruth.org/agape-love.html

Acknowledgements

I want to take the time to acknowledge several people who God placed in my life that encouraged and inspired me to write a second book.

First, I want to acknowledge my Mother, my Father, my Step-in Mother, my older brother Tony and my older sister Tanya for their prayers and support. They have inspired me to keep my light shining.

Second, I want to acknowledge a very special spiritual mother who from the moment I finished, *The Book of Prayers for the Seasons of Life*, encouraged me to write a second book, Exhorter Danita Mosley.

Last, I want to acknowledge the churches that I have pastored, Beulah African Methodist Episcopal Church in Farmville, VA and St. Paul A.M.E. Church, Danville, VA.

Thank you for reading and supporting *Keep your Life Lit*! I hope it blessed your life!

Journaling Pages

www.ingramcontent.com/pod-product-compliance
Lightning Source LLC
Chambersburg PA
CBHW071318080526
44587CB00018B/3267